Dɪsnᴇp · PIXAR

INCREDIBLES 2

THE OFFICIAL GUIDE

DISNEY · PIXAR

INCREDIBLES 2

THE OFFICIAL GUIDE

WRITTEN BY MATT JONES, RUTH AMOS AND JULIA MARCH

CONTENTS

The Parrs are definitely not a typical family. From invisibility to super-strength, each of them has an amazing Super power. Sometimes they get along and other times they argue – but the Parrs are always ready to unite as the crime-fighting team known as the Incredibles!

DASH

VIOLET

JACK-JACK

ELASTIGIRL

Aka Helen Parr

Elastigirl is a powerful, fast and very flexible Super. She is super-stretchy, super-clever and an incredible mum, too!

THINGS YOU NEED TO KNOW ABOUT ELASTIGIRL

1 She can stretch any part of her body up to 30 m (100 ft)!

2 Elastigirl is a great pilot.

3 She can take the shape of a parachute, trampoline or catapult.

4 People adore Elastigirl, and often chant her name.

8

BACK IN ACTION

After a business meeting with Winston and Evelyn Deavor, Elastigirl joins their plan to make Supers legal again. She has to move away from her family, and restart her crime-fighting career.

AWAY FROM HOME

The Deavors book a posh hotel suite for Helen to stay in while she is fighting crime in New Urbem. There, she can relax and unwind after her busy day being a Superhero.

BEST FOR THE JOB

According to Evelyn's maths calculations, Elastigirl is the ideal choice to become a Superhero again. She causes a lot less damage than Mr Incredible!

NEW OUTFIT

Elastigirl gets a new Supersuit, designed by Alexander Galbaki. This suit looks really cool, but Helen isn't sure if it's her style.

ELASTICYCLE

The Deavors give Elastigirl a custom-made vehicle for her new mission. Evelyn personally designed this high-tech bike!

DID YOU KNOW?

Elastigirl has ridden bikes for years. She also used to have a Mohican hairstyle!

Computer
screen

SUPER FEATURE

The Elasticycle can break up
into two unicycles, and Elastigirl
can stretch between them!

Elastigirl's
logo

PARACHUTE
Floats down to the ground safely, slowing the fall.

STRETCHING UP BETWEEN BUILDINGS
Quickly manoeuvres herself upwards.

UNLOCKING DOORS FROM THE INSIDE
Useful for entering villains' lairs.

ROOFTOP STRETCH
Easier than jumping!

SUPER ARM STRETCH
Helps with using tracker devices to hunt down foes.

SUPER-FLEXI STRETCHES

Flexible Elastigirl uses her powers to dodge hazards and chase criminals. Twisting, turning, winding and leaping – villains better beware this bendy Super!

DID YOU KNOW?

Elastigirl can stretch her legs to kick villains that are far away from her.

TRAMPOLINE

Allows others to bounce off her in pursuit of villains.

THINGS YOU NEED TO KNOW ABOUT MR INCREDIBLE

1 He can punch through brick, concrete and metal.

2 Mr Incredible can lift heavy objects with ease – even vehicles.

3 He is highly resistant to injury.

4 He often causes accidental damage to buildings and vehicles!

MR INCREDIBLE

Aka Bob Parr

Mr Incredible is fast, fit and very, very strong. A super husband and dad, he is as devoted to his family as he is to saving the world.

STAY-AT-HOME DAD

When Helen becomes a Superhero again, Bob has to look after the kids by himself. He wishes he could be a Superhero too, but he has nappies to change!

1
Feed the kids a good breakfast!

BOB'S CHECKLIST
Bob has a long list of jobs to do!

2

Make sure Violet and Dash don't miss the school bus.

3

Tell Violet she must be home by 10:30 p.m. after her date with Tony Rydinger.

4 Read to Jack-Jack before bed and make sure he drinks his milk.

5 Help Dash with his maths homework.

6 Don't let Jack-Jack watch TV when he should be sleeping!

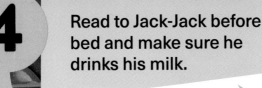

NEW MATH
for Life

$5x = 10 - 3x$
$5x + 3x = 10$
$8x = 10$
$\dfrac{8x}{8} = \dfrac{10}{8}$ $x = \dfrac{10}{8}$

"I've got this. Everything's GREAT."

Mr Incredible

7 Don't panic – tell Helen everything is fine.

8 Make sure the children actually sleep in their beds.

VIOLET

Incredible daughter

Violet Parr was once shy, but she is now a confident Super. Creating force fields and turning invisible are her special powers.

THINGS YOU NEED TO KNOW ABOUT VIOLET PARR

1 Violet and her brother Dash often fight.

2 She is incredibly intelligent, and can work out a solution to any problem.

3 She has a major crush on her classmate Tony Rydinger.

4 Vi doesn't always get along with her father, but still thinks he is a super dad!

VIOLET VS SUPERSUIT

She tries to tear it
apart with her teeth.
RESULT: Suit unmarked

2

Violet discovers that the boy she likes has had his mind wiped – all thanks to her dad. She takes her anger out on her Supersuit!

1 She stuffs the suit in the sink disposal unit.
RESULT: Suit unharmed

3 She throws it against a brick wall.
RESULT: Suit undamaged

WHO WINS?
Supersuit: Winner
Violet: Loser

25

DASH

Speedy son

Dashiell Parr does everything at top speed. Well, maybe not his homework! He's the fastest Super ever, and can even run on water.

THINGS YOU NEED TO KNOW ABOUT DASH PARR

1 Dash struggles to keep the secret that he is a Super.

2 He always wants to be right in the middle of the action.

3 Sometimes Dash forgets to wash his hands. Yuck!

4 He hates vegetables, even though they are good for him.

DASH'S FAVOURITE THINGS

Dash loves to use his Super power and hates having to hide it. There are lots more activities that this energy-filled Super likes, too!

EATING BREAKFAST

Sugar Bombs and waffles are the best.

EMBARRASSING VIOLET

Dash loudly introduces himself to her crush!

PRESSING MYSTERIOUS BUTTONS ON REMOTES

It's fun to fire the Incredibile's rocket jets and control the house's underfloor streams.

FAMILY CRIME-FIGHTING

It's cool to take on the bad guys together.

FINISHING HIS HOMEWORK

Then, Dash can go and play!

RUNNING

Being a blur is awesome.

DUELLING WITH HYPNOTISED SUPERS

Let the fight begin!

JACK-JACK

Talented tot

Baby Jack-Jack is the youngest child in the family. At first, the Parrs think he has no Super powers. In fact, he has more than all of them combined!

THINGS YOU NEED TO KNOW ABOUT JACK-JACK PARR

1 If he can grab the TV remote, he always chooses an old crime movie.

2 A cookie never fails to bring Jack-Jack out of hiding.

3 He enjoys listening to Mozart.

4 He doesn't trust raccoons one little bit!

JACK-JACK'S AMAZING POWERS

Although Jack-Jack can't speak yet, this Super child can do far more than a normal baby. Perhaps only Jack-Jack knows just how many Super powers he has!

LASER EYES
Duck! Jack-Jack can shoot green lasers from his eyes!

PHASING

Jack-Jack is able to pass through any object, like a ghost.

FIRE STARTER

Jack-Jack can set himself on fire, and anything that he is holding.

DID YOU KNOW?
Jack-Jack can grow in size to become a giant baby!

"No firing the baby around the house."

Mr Incredible to Dash and Violet

COPYCAT
Jack-Jack can change his appearance to look exactly like another person.

TELEPORTATION
Jack-Jack is able to vanish from one place and instantly reappear in another!

"Any solution involving cookies will inevitably result in the demon baby."
Edna Mode

DID YOU KNOW? Jack-Jack can even make himself gooey, so that things stick to him. Yuck!

MONSTER BABY
Jack-Jack can turn himself into a scary monster!

MULTIPLYING
Jack-Jack can create many copies of himself. He is quite a handful!

THINGS YOU NEED TO KNOW ABOUT FROZONE

1 Frozone can shoot ice from his hands.

2 His shoes can turn into skis, ice skates or even a disc to ride on.

3 He once retired as a Super, but kept his Supersuit just in case.

4 Frozone's wife, Honey, does not have any Super powers.

FROZONE

Aka Lucius Best

Frozone is an ally of Mr Incredible and a friend to all the Parrs. His icy powers have got the Incredibles out of hot water time and again!

WHICH SUPER ARE YOU?

It's time to test what type of incredible Superhero you are!

1

HOW WOULD YOU DESCRIBE YOUR PERSONALITY?
A) Chilled
B) Adventurous
C) Fun

2

WHAT'S YOUR FAVOURITE METHOD OF TRANSPORTION?
A) Cool car
B) Motorcycle
C) Pushchair

3

WHAT'S YOUR FAVOURITE SNACK?
A) Ice cream
B) Vegetables
C) Cookies

4

WHAT'S YOUR BEST QUALITY?
A) Loyalty
B) Determination
C) Creativity

5

YOU NEED TO TRAVEL QUICKLY FROM ONE BUILDING TO ANOTHER. HOW DO YOU DO IT?
A) Build an ice bridge out of thin air.
B) Stretch between the gap.
C) Disappear and then reappear in the other building.

Mostly As – Frozone
Like Frozone, you're super cool. You remain calm in the face of danger and you're very loyal to your friends.

Mostly Bs – Elastigirl
Like Elastigirl, you're brave and clever. You're determined to always try your best, whatever happens.

Mostly Cs – Jack-Jack
Like Jack-Jack, you're a bundle of fun! You're creative and unpredictable – people never know what you'll do next!

40

THE UNDERMINER

Tunnelling terror

Beware the Underminer! This mole-like villain robs Municiberg's bank vaults. He then drills up to the surface to cause chaos in the city. Will he get away with it?

THINGS YOU NEED TO KNOW ABOUT THE UNDERMINER

1 He drives a Tunneller vehicle with an enormous drill at the front.

2 His hands are metal, and he calls them JACK and HAMMER.

3 His underground explosives cause an entire city block to collapse.

4 He could use a good dentist!

DARING BANK HEIST

The Underminer has carefully planned out his raid on Municiberg's banks, but he isn't expecting to face Frozone and the Incredibles!

TUNNELLER CHAOS

The Incredibles and Frozone work together to stop the Tunneller from destroying Municiberg's City Hall.

DID YOU KNOW?

The Underminer grumpily declares war on peace and happiness.

“All will tremble before me!”

The Underminer

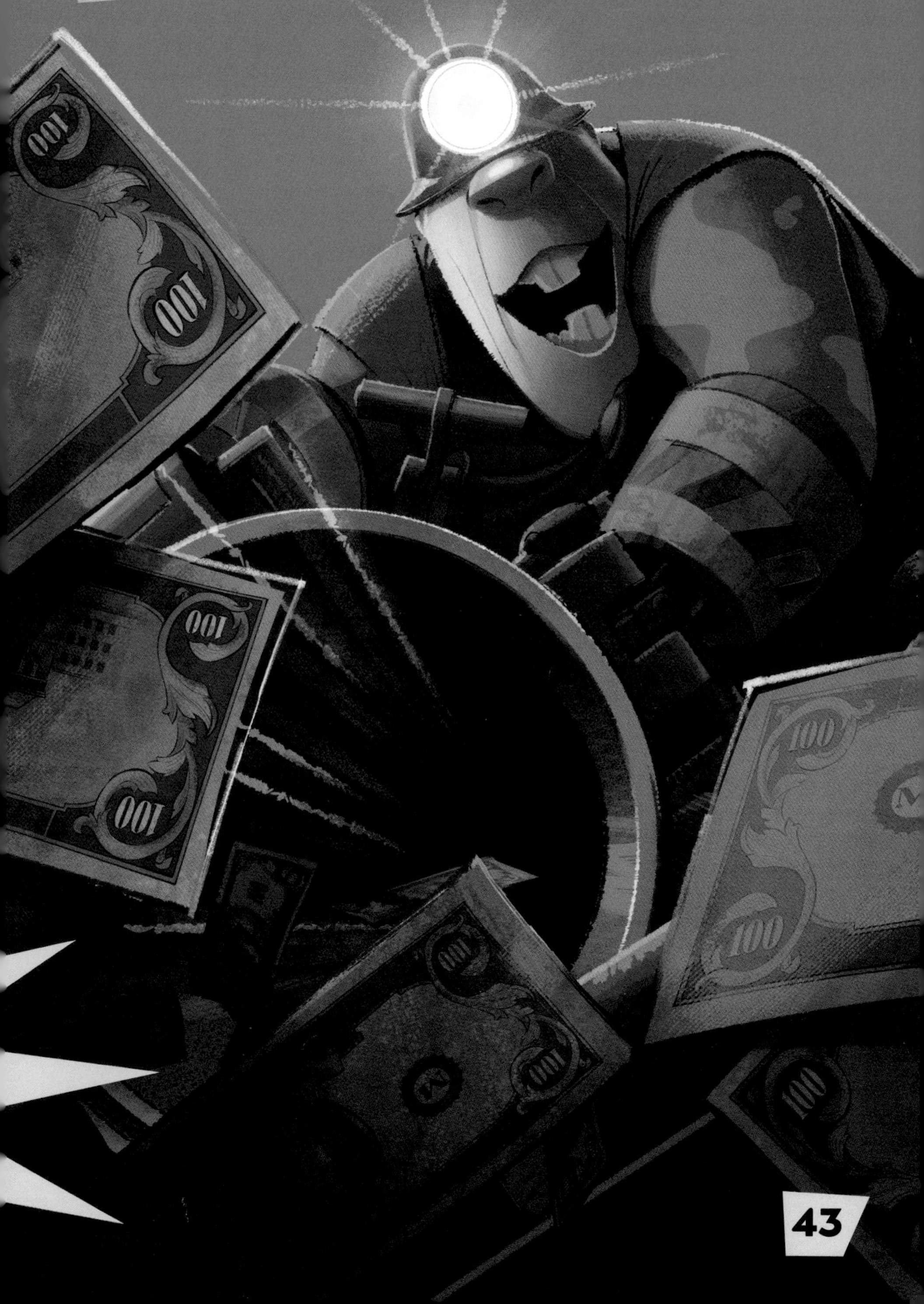

RICK DICKER
Super supporter

Rick works for the Supers Relocation Programme, helping Supers to live normal lives. For years, this loyal agent has done all he can to help the Incredibles stay undercover.

THINGS YOU NEED TO KNOW ABOUT RICK DICKER

1 It's Rick's job to wipe the memory of anyone who learns a Super's identity.

2 Rick has been friends with Elastigirl, Mr Incredible and Frozone for years.

3 Poor Rick loses his job when the Supers Relocation Programme is closed.

4 Rick accidentally wipes all traces of Violet from Tony Rydinger's mind!

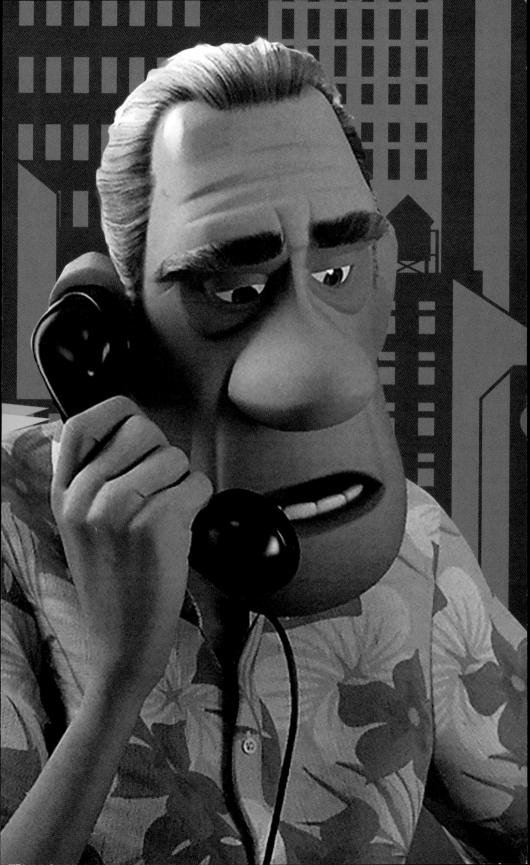

THINGS YOU NEED TO KNOW ABOUT TONY

1 Tony is shocked when he sees Violet in her Supersuit, but he soon forgets about it when his mind is wiped!

2 He asks Violet out on a date – then stands her up when Rick makes him forget all about it. Oops!

3 Tony has a mirror in his locker, so he can check he is still looking cool.

4 Tony loves music, and is a member of the school choir.

TONY RYDINGER

Violet's crush

Tony is Violet's classmate and crush at Western View Junior High. He's a popular, sporty teen who secretly likes Violet back – although he tries to play it cool!

WINSTON

Supers' biggest fan

Winston Deavor is a superfan of all Supers. This rich businessman has a plan to make them legal again – and it's a super clever one!

THINGS YOU NEED TO KNOW ABOUT WINSTON

1 He owns mansions, fancy cars, a private jet and a high-tech yacht.

2 At one time, Rick Dicker was Winston's boss!

3 He knows lots of Supers' theme tunes by heart.

4 Winston and his sister own a company called DevTech.

THINGS YOU NEED TO KNOW ABOUT EVELYN

1 She loves Winston, but she often doesn't agree with him.

2 She designed Elastigirl's new vehicle and the camera in her suit.

3 Evelyn is responsible for developing all the technology for DevTech.

4 She's so friendly that Elastigirl finds it easy to open up to her.

EVELYN

Extraordinary inventor

Evelyn Deavor founded DevTech with her brother, Winston. She's fun, brilliant and knows everything about technology. Clever Evelyn soon gains Elastigirl's trust.

THE DEAVORS' SUPER PLAN

Winston and Evelyn have a great scheme to make Supers legal again. It will just take a little amazing technology, some Super action and a lot of positive publicity!

Put a tiny camera onto Elastigirl's Supersuit.

1

2

ELASTIGIRL RESCUES HUNDREDS

Get Elastigirl back in action, fighting crime.

"KA-BOOM! KA-POW! SUPERS SHOULD BE LEGAL NOW!"

Bystander chant

3 Record action footage of her saving the day.

4 Show the footage to the public to gain their support.

5 Persuade politicians that Supers are incredible.

6 Get politicians to make Supers legal again. Hooray!

INCREDIBLE NEW HOUSE!

The Parrs' new home is a modern mansion on top of a hill above Municiberg. The Incredibles are really excited, as the house is so much better than the small motel they were staying in!

DID YOU KNOW?

Winston owns the mansion, and he lets the Parrs live there as long as they want – and for free, too!

Large balcony

SPECIAL FEATURES
An eccentric billionaire built the house,
so it has lots of cool, secret areas. The garage's
exit is hidden behind a flowing waterfall.

"Wicked cool!"
Dash

Luxurious pool

HOME, SWEET HOME

The inside of the mansion is just as impressive as the outside. There are indoor waterfalls, plants and beautiful pieces of furniture and art.

LET'S GET COOKING

The kitchen is fully stocked with food and has all the latest gadgets. The kids eat their breakfast at the bar with a great view of the garden.

UNPACKING

Bob is so busy looking after the kids that he hasn't fully unpacked yet. His new den is full of boxes of mementos from his days as a Super.

DID YOU KNOW?

There are several remote-controlled water features under the floor. Bob falls into one!

JACK-JACK VS RACCOON

Intruder alert! Jack-Jack spots a criminal raccoon stealing chicken legs from the rubbish. Inspired by his family, this baby is not going to let the robber get away with it!

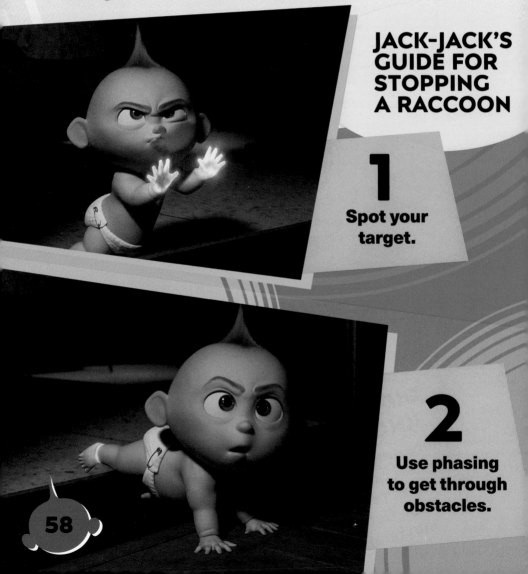

JACK-JACK'S GUIDE FOR STOPPING A RACCOON

1

Spot your target.

2

Use phasing to get through obstacles.

3

Size up your opponent.

4

Start fighting!

DID YOU KNOW?

Jack-Jack confuses the raccoon with a masked robber from a classic movie on TV.

THE FIGHT CONTINUES...

5

Get yourself fired up!

6

Trap your foe.

7

Cut off your enemy's escape routes.

8

Gang up on your target.

9

Watch the intruder slink away.

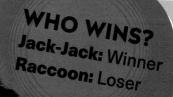

WHO WINS?
Jack-Jack: Winner
Raccoon: Loser

61

NEW URBEM

New Urbem is a modern, buzzing city, but it also has a dark side. Daring criminals lurk here, so it is the perfect place for Elastigirl to be a Superhero again.

"It's like a Superheroes' playground!"
Winston Deavor

DARING RESCUE

Above New Urbem, the Screenslaver hijacks a helicopter carrying an important ambassador. Elastigirl has to swing into action to save her!

THE METROLEV

This high-tech train is the fastest way to get around New Urbem. It speeds along, hovering above the train tracks. Will the MetroLev's first ever journey go to plan?

Luxurious passenger coaches

DID YOU KNOW?
New Urbem's mayor organises a big party to celebrate the MetroLev's first trip. He even hires a band.

RUNAWAY TRAIN

As soon as the MetroLev departs, it zooms off backwards! Everyone panics, but luckily Elastigirl keeps her cool. She chases it on her Elasticycle and rescues the passengers.

Engineer's cabin

THE SCREENSLAVER

High-tech hypnotist

The sinister Screenslaver is hijacking technology everywhere! This creepy villain can hypnotise anyone, anywhere, using any screen! Who could it be?

THINGS YOU NEED TO KNOW ABOUT THE SCREENSLAVER

1 This villain hypnotises victims using television screens.

2 The Screenslaver's costume includes a scary mask with giant goggles.

3 The Screenslaver thinks humans are lazy and gladly let others run their lives.

4 This horrible hypnotist seems to know an awful lot about Elastigirl!

THE SCREENSLAVER'S LAIR

Elastigirl tracks the Screenslaver to his creepy flat. This mysterious den is filled with curious tools and gadgets for hypnotising people.

Spooky eyeball

NORMAL BLOCK

Unlike other villains, the Screenslaver does not have a lair on a remote tropical island. He tinkers away in a flat in New Urbem.

Mysterious diagram

EDNA
Super designer

Edna Mode fuses fashion and technology to create costumes for the Supers she adores. Edna may be petite, but she has a big reputation to uphold, darling!

THINGS YOU NEED TO KNOW ABOUT EDNA MODE

1 Making hero-wear is her great passion, but she also designs high-fashion bags.

2 Once she discovers his powers, "Auntie Edna" is happy to babysit Jack-Jack anytime.

3 Edna finds that listening to Mozart helps her creative juices to flow.

4 Her sharp words can be as cutting as her scissors!

EDNA'S HOUSE

Edna lives in a modern, glass mansion that she has tailored to her tastes. It sits on top of a grassy hill and is surrounded by state-of-the-art security systems, including a laser-gate!

Statue in modern art style

Floor-to-ceiling glass windows

Cubed hedges

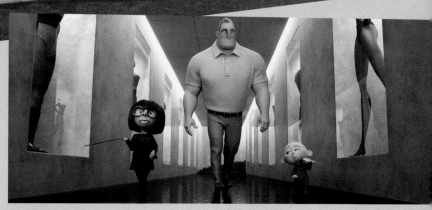

HALL OF FAME

Edna keeps some of her favourite Supersuit designs on mannequins in the hallway that leads to her studio.

"I AM NOT A BABY PERSON, ROBERT! I HAVE NO BABY FACILITIES!"

Edna Mode

JACK-JACK'S BRAND NEW SUPERSUIT

The last Supersuit that Edna made for Jack-Jack was only fireproof and bulletproof. The new suit needs even more special features to help control Jack-Jack's multiple powers.

SUPER FEATURES

Edna makes the suit out of high-tech fabrics. It has many tiny sensors that detect which power the baby will use next. The sensors then alert Mr Incredible, via a monitor.

Suit's edible flame-retardant foam is lavender and blackberry flavour

DID YOU KNOW?
Edna demands to be the exclusive Supersuit designer for Elastigirl, Mr Incredible and Frozone from now until the end of time!

Space for Jack-Jack's nappy

THE HAPPY PLATTER

Tony works part-time as a waiter at The Happy Platter. When the Parrs turn up, the kids don't realise that Bob is trying to reignite the romance between Tony and Violet. Vi is so embarrassed!

DID YOU KNOW?

Bob enjoys the water served at The Happy Platter. He finds it ever so refreshing.

FAMILY PLACE

The Happy Platter is a popular restaurant in Municiberg. It is owned by Tony's family and has a relaxed, friendly vibe.

WANNABE

VOYD AND HE-LECTRIX

Inspired by Elastigirl, other Supers want to become heroes. The Deavors organise them into a Super group. Voyd and He-lectrix are just two of these powerful wannabes.

VOYD
Voyd is a shy Super and a big fan of Elastigirl. She makes portals, which can transfer people or objects from one place to another.

SUPERS

At a DevTech party, Voyd and He-lectrix slow dance together. Are there sparks between them?

HE-LECTRIX

This stylish Super can generate electricity. He zaps bad guys with lightning bolts!

SCREECH AND REFLUX

These two wannabe Supers have awesome abilities, thanks to their unusual bodies. When they join Winston's crew, they can't wait to meet Elastigirl – a real Superhero!

REFLUX

This kind Super has a terrible tummy. He can spew lava from his mouth!

SCREECH

This Super has huge, feathery wings. He flies like an owl and screeches like one, too!

DID YOU KNOW?

Screech considers Elastigirl to be a great role model for other Supers.

KRUSHAUER AND BRICK

These hulking wannabe Supers are not big on words. Instead, they rely on their astonishing Super powers to make an impression!

KRUSHAUER

Krushauer loves to crush things. He can do it with his hands, but he can also use just his mind.

BRICK

This Super can expand her body so that she becomes as big and strong as a brick wall!

DID YOU KNOW?

Don't ask Krushauer to uncrush things. He just can't understand why anyone would want to.

THE INCREDIBILE

This gadget-packed vehicle used to be Bob's car when he was a Superhero. He thought the Incredibile had been destroyed, but he sees it on TV in perfect condition!

Ejector seat

Rocket turbine thruster

DID YOU KNOW?

When the wannabe Supers attack the Parrs, Dash summons the Incredibile to help them escape.

REMOTE CONTROL

Bob still has the Incredibile remote, packed away in a moving box. Using the remote, anyone can control the car from far away!

Pair of hidden rocket launchers

"INCREDIBILE!
SET VOICE
IDENTIFICATION!"

Frozone

89

THE *EVERJUST*

The Deavors own a magnificent boat called the *EVERJUST*. More than 100 world leaders gather on it for a meeting to make Supers legal again! What could possibly go wrong?

Hydrofoil allows boat to skim on top of water

DID YOU KNOW?
The roof of this huge ship is actually a detachable jet plane!

Helicopter pad

HEIGHT OF LUXURY

Like everything the Deavors own, this yacht is expensive and elegant – and it's the fastest ship on the planet! It has a grand staircase and a huge ballroom where guests can dance.

WHAT'S YOUR SUPER POWER?

From invisibility to great strength, Superheroes have many different types of powers! Which one would you be most likely to have?

Do you sometimes feel shy?

No

Yes

START

Are you a bit of a show-off?

Are you good at coping with stress?

No

Yes

Are you often rushing around?

Yes

No

SUPER-SPEED
Running at a really quick speed

ICE POWERS
Shooting beams of ice from your hands

CRUSHING POWERS
Squashing objects with your mind

No

ELASTICITY
Stretching your body to incredible lengths and into impossible shapes

Can you adapt to difficult situations?

No

Yes

INVISIBILITY
Becoming completely see-through

Do you often take shortcuts?

No

Yes

CREATING PORTALS
Transporting objects or people between places

Yes

SUPERPOWERED TANTRUMS
Shooting laser eye beams, duplicating yourself, turning into a monster baby

No

Are you good at unscrewing jar lids?

Yes

SUPER-STRENGTH
Never having to worry about carrying something too heavy again

"WE KNOW! FIGHT NOW, TALK LATER!"

Mr Incredible

Penguin
Random
House

Project Editor Ruth Amos
Senior Designer Lynne Moulding
Editors Matt Jones and Julia March
Designer Ian Midson
Pre-production Producer Siu Yin Chan
Producer Zara Markland
Managing Editor Sadie Smith
Managing Art Editor Vicky Short
Publisher Julie Ferris
Art Director Lisa Lanzarini
Publishing Director Simon Beecroft

First published in Great Britain in 2018 by
Dorling Kindersley Limited
80 Strand, London WC2R 0RL
A Penguin Random House Company

10 9 8 7 6 5 4 3 2 1

002–306330–June/2018
Page design copyright © 2018 Dorling Kindersley Limited

A CIP catalogue record for this book
is available from the British Library.

ISBN: 978-0-24130-487-7

Printed and bound in Slovakia

A WORLD OF IDEAS:
SEE ALL THERE IS TO KNOW

www.dk.com
www.disney.com